Little Snow by The Brother with Annotations

Includes the following Annotations:
Introduction,
Key Themes, Snow White's Character,
The Queen's Character, The Seven
Dwarf's Characters, Summary of the
Story, The Brothers Grimm's Techniques
– Form and Structure, About the
Authors 'The Brothers Grimm' and
Glossary of Literary Terms
by Classic Literature Annotated

You're invited to check out
and follow
'Classic Literature Annotated'
by Katie Louise Durie
please scan the QR code below
for more information:

Little Snow White
By The Brothers Grimm
with Annotations

Includes the following Annotations:
Introduction,
Key Themes, Snow White's Character,
The Queen's Character, The Seven
Dwarf's Characters, Summary of the
Story, The Brothers Grimm's Techniques
– Form and Structure, About the
Authors 'The Brothers Grimm' and
Glossary of Literary Terms
by Classic Literature Annotated

All Annotations Copyright 2025,
Katie Louise Durie, owner of
Classic Literature Annotated
All Rights Reserved

*'Little Snow White' was Originally
Published in 1812*

CHARACTERS

Main Characters:

Snow White – The protagonist, a beautiful and innocent young princess whose appearance – skin as white as snow, lips as red as blood, and hair as black as ebony – makes her the target of her stepmother's jealousy. Her kindness, purity, and resilience define her character.

The Queen (Stepmother) – The main antagonist, Snow White's vain and jealous stepmother. Obsessed with being the fairest of them all, she repeatedly tries to kill Snow White out of envy.

The Magic Mirror – A mystical mirror that tells the truth about who is the fairest in the land. It serves as a symbol of truth and the queen's vanity, driving much of the conflict.

The Seven Dwarfs – Kind and hardworking miners who find Snow White in their cottage and protect her. They offer her refuge and warn her of the dangers posed by the queen.

The Prince – A noble figure who falls in love with Snow White after discovering her in the glass coffin. His love and intervention (accidentally dislodging the poisoned apple) revive Snow White, leading to their marriage.

The King (Snow White's Father) – Although he plays a minimal role in the story, the king's remarriage to the queen sets the plot in motion. His absence after marrying the queen is notable.

The Huntsman – A servant of the queen, tasked with killing Snow White. Moved by her innocence, he spares her life and deceives the queen by presenting a boar's heart instead.

Minor Characters:

Forest Animals – The creatures of the forest, often seen as part of the setting, who indirectly help Snow White by not harming her when she is abandoned.

The Dwarfs' Animals and Birds – Symbolic mourners when Snow White is thought to be dead. A dove, raven, and owl are mentioned as paying respect at her glass coffin.

CONTENTS

Introduction 6

Little Snow White 7

Key Themes 18

Snow White's Character 20

The Queen's Character 22

The Seven Dwarf's Characters 24

Summary of the story 26

The Brothers Grimm's Techniques
– Form and Structure 28

Glossary of Literary Terms 32

About the Authors
'The Brothers Grimm' 34

INTRODUCTION

"Little Snow White" is a classic fairy tale created by the Brothers Grimm, first published in 1812. It tells the story of a young princess whose extraordinary beauty provokes the jealousy of her vain and wicked stepmother, the queen. Driven by envy, the queen repeatedly tries to eliminate Snow White, leading to a series of perilous encounters that test the princess's innocence and resilience.

Set against the backdrop of enchanted forests, magical mirrors, and a cottage inhabited by seven dwarfs, the tale explores timeless themes of jealousy, vanity, kindness, and the triumph of good over evil. Snow White's journey from danger to salvation reflects the enduring power of love, compassion, and inner beauty.

The story's rich symbolism, from the poisoned apple to the glass coffin, has captivated audiences for centuries, inspiring countless adaptations in literature, film, and art. As one of the most beloved fairy tales, *"Little Snow White"* continues to resonate across generations, embodying the universal battle between light and darkness.

LITTLE SNOW WHITE

It was in the middle of winter, when the broad flakes of snow were falling around, that a certain queen sat working at her window, the frame of which was made of fine black ebony; and, as she was looking out upon the snow, she pricked her finger, and three drops of blood fell upon it. Then she gazed thoughtfully down on the red drops which sprinkled the white snow and said, "Would that my little daughter may be as white as that snow, as red as the blood, and as black as the ebony window-frame!" And so the little girl grew up; her skin was a white as snow, her cheeks as rosy as blood, and her hair as black as ebony; and she was called Snow-White.

But this queen died; and the king soon married another wife, who was very beautiful, but so proud that she could not bear to think that any one could surpass her. She had a magical looking-glass, to which she used to go and gaze upon herself in it, and say—

"Tell me, glass, tell me true!

Of all the ladies in the land,

Who is fairest? Tell me who?"

And the glass answered, "Thou, Queen, art fairest in the land".

But Snow-White grew more and more beautiful; and when she was seven years old, she was as bright as the day, and fairer than the queen herself. Then the glass one day answered queen, when she went to consult it as usual —

"Thou, Queen, may'st fair and beauteous be,

But Snow-White is lovelier far than thee."

When the queen heard this she turned pale with rage and envy; and calling to one of her servants said, "Take Snow-White away into the wide wood, that I may never see her more." Then the servant led the little girl away; but his heart melted when she begged him to spare her life, and he said, "I will not hurt thee, thou pretty child." So he left her there alone; and though he thought it most likely that the wild beasts would tear her to pieces, he felt as if a great weight were taken off his heart when he had made up his mind not to kill her, but leave her to her fate.

Then poor Snow-White wandered along through the wood in great fear; and the wild beasts roared around, but none did her any harm. In the evening she came to a little cottage, and went in there to rest, for her weary feet would carry her no further. Everything was spruce and neat in the cottage: on the table was spread a white cloth, and there were seven little plates with seven little loaves and seven little glasses with wine in them; and knives and forks laid in order, and by the wall stood seven little beds. Then, as she was exceedingly hungry, she picked a little piece off each loaf, and drank a very little wine out of each glass; and after that she thought she would lie down and rest. So she tried all the little beds; and one was too long, and another was too short, till, at last, the seventh suited her; and there she laid herself down and went to sleep. Presently in came the masters of the cottage, who were seven little dwarfs that lived among the mountains, and dug and searched about for gold. They lighted up their seven lamps, and saw directly that all was not right. The first said, "Who has been sitting on my stool?" The second, "Who has been eating off my plate?" The third, "Who has been picking at my bread?" The fourth, "Who has been meddling with my spoon?" The fifth, "Who has been handling my fork?" The sixth, "Who has been cutting with my knife?" The seventh, "Who has been drinking my wine?" Then the first looked around and said, "Who has been lying on my bed?" And the rest came running to him, and every one cried out that somebody had been upon his bed. But the seventh saw Snow-White, and called upon his brethren to come and look at her; and they cried out with wonder and astonishment, and brought their lamps and gazing upon her, they said, "Good heavens! What a lovely child she is!" And they were delighted to see her, and took care not to waken her; and the seventh dwarf slept an hour with each of the other dwarfs in turn, till the night was gone.

In the morning Snow-White told them all her story, and they pitied her, and said if she would keep all things in order, and cook and wash, and knit and spin for them, she might stay where she was, and they would take good care of her. Then they went out all day long to their work, seeking for gold and silver in the mountains; and Snow-White remained at home; and they warned her, saying, "The queen will soon find out where you are, so take care and let no one in." But the queen, now that she thought Snow-White was dead, believed that she was certainly the handsomest lady in the land; so she went to her glass and said —

"Tell me, glass, tell me true!

Of all the ladies in the land,

Who is fairest? tell me who?"

And the glass answered —

"Thou, Queen, thou are fairest in all this land;

But over the Hills, in the greenwood shade,

Where the seven dwarfs their dwelling have made,

There Snow-White is hiding; and she

Is lovelier far, O Queen, than thee."

Then the queen was very much alarmed; for she knew that the glass always spoke the truth, and she was sure that the servant had betrayed her. And as she could not bear to think that any one lived who was more beautiful than she was, she disguised herself as an old pedlar woman and went her way over the hills to the place where the dwarfs dwelt. Then she knocked at the door and cried, "Fine wares to sell!" Snow-White looked out of the window, and said, "Good day, good woman; what have you to sell?" "Good wares, fine wares," replied she; "laces and bobbins of all colors." "I will let the old lady in; she seems to be a very good sort of a body," thought Snow-White; so she ran down, and unbolted the door. "Bless me!" said the woman, "how badly your stays are laced. Let me lace them up with one of my nice new laces." Snow-White did not dream of any mischief; so she stood up before the old woman who set to work so nimbly, and pulled the lace so tightly that Snow-White lost her breath, and fell down as if she were dead. "There's an end of all thy beauty," said the spiteful queen, and went away home.

In the evening the seven dwarfs returned; and I need not say how grieved they were to see their faithful Snow-White stretched upon the ground motionless, as if she were quite dead. However, they lifted her up, and when they found what was the matter, they cut the lace; and in a little time she began to breathe, and soon came to herself again. Then they said, "The old woman was the queen; take care another time, and let no one in when we are away."

When the queen got home, she went to her glass, and spoke to it, but to her surprise it replied in the same words as before.

Then the blood ran cold in her heart with spite and malice to hear that Snow-White still lived; and she dressed herself up again in a disguise, but very different from the one she wore before, and took with her a poisoned comb. When she reached the dwarfs' cottage, she knocked at the door, and cried, "Fine wares to sell!" but Snow-White said, "I dare not let any one in." Then the queen said, "Only look at my beautiful combs;" and gave her the poisoned one. And it looked so pretty that the little girl took it up and put it into her hair to try it; but the moment it touched her head the poison was so powerful that she fell down senseless. "There you may lie," said the queen, and went her way. But by good luck the dwarfs returned very early that evening; and when they saw Snow-White lying on the ground, they thought what had happened, and soon found the poisoned comb. And when they took it away, she recovered, and told them all that had passed; and they warned her once more not to open the door to any one.

Meantime the queen went home to her glass, and trembled with rage when she received exactly the same answer as before; and she said, "Snow-White shall die, if it costs me my life." So she went secretly into a chamber, and prepared a poisoned apple: the outside looked very rosy and tempting, but whosoever tasted it was sure to die. Then she dressed herself up as a peasant's wife, and travelled over the hills to the dwarfs' cottage, and knocked at the door; but Snow-White put her head out of the window, and said, "I dare not let any one in, for the dwarfs have told me not to." "Do as you please," said the old woman, "but at any rate take this pretty apple; I will make you a present of it." "No," said Snow-White, "I dare not take it." "You silly girl!" answered the other, "what are you afraid of? Do you think it is poisoned? Come! You eat one part, and I will eat the other." Now the apple was so prepared that one side was good, though the other side was poisoned. Then Snow-White was very much tempted to taste, for the apple looked exceedingly nice; and when she saw the old woman eat, she could refrain no longer. But she had scarcely put the piece into her mouth when she fell down dead upon the ground. "This time nothing will save thee," said the queen; and she went home to her glass, and at last it said—"Thou, Queen, art the fairest of all the fair." And then her envious heart was glad, and as happy as such a heart could be.

When evening came, and the dwarfs returned home, they found Snow-White lying on the ground; no breath passed her lips, and they were afraid that she was quite dead. They lifted her up, and combed her hair, and washed her face with wine and water; but all was in vain. So they laid her down upon a bier, and all seven watched and bewailed her three whole days; and then they proposed to bury her; but her cheeks were still rosy, and her face looked just as it did while she was alive; so they said, "We will never bury her in the cold ground." And they made a coffin of glass so that they might still look at her, and wrote her name upon it in golden letters, and that she was a king's daughter. Then the coffin was placed upon the hill, and one of the dwarfs always sat by it and watched. And the birds of the air came, too, and bemoaned Snow-White. First of all came an owl, and then a raven, but at last came a dove.

And thus Snow-White lay for a long, long time, and still only looked as though she were asleep; for she was even now as white as snow, and as red as blood, and as black as ebony. At last a prince came and called at the dwarfs' house; and he saw Snow-White and read what was written in golden letters. Then he offered the dwarfs money, and earnestly prayed them to let him take her away; but they said, "We will not part with her for all the gold in the world." At last, however, they had pity on him, and gave him the coffin; but the moment he lifted it up to carry it home with him, the piece of apple fell from between her lips, and Snow-White awoke, and exclaimed, "Where am I!" And the prince answered, "Thou art safe with me." Then he told her all that had happened, and said, "I love you better than all the world; come with me to my father's palace, and you shall be my wife." Snow-White consented, and went home with the prince; and everything was prepared with great pomp and splendor for their wedding.

To the feast was invited, among the rest, Snow-White's old enemy, the queen; and as she was dressing herself in fine, rich clothes, she looked in the glass and said, "Tell me, glass, tell me true! Of all the ladies in the land, who is fairest? Tell me who?" And the glass answered, "Thou, lady, art the loveliest *here*, I ween; But lovelier far is the new-made queen."

When she heard this, the queen started with rage; but her envy and curiosity were so great, that she could not help setting out to see the bride. And when she arrived, and saw that it was no other than Snow-White, whom she thought had been dead a long while, she choked with passion, and fell ill and died; but Snow-White and the prince lived and reigned happily over that land, many, many years.

KEY THEMES

Jealousy and Envy – The queen's obsession with being the fairest in the land drives her to attempt to kill Snow White multiple times. This theme highlights the destructive nature of envy and vanity.

Innocence and Purity – Snow White is characterized by her innocence and beauty, which contrast sharply with the queen's malice. Her purity ultimately shields her, symbolizing the triumph of good over evil.

Deception and Disguise – The queen disguises herself to deceive Snow White, illustrating how evil often masks itself to achieve its goals.

Kindness and Compassion – The dwarfs' willingness to protect Snow White reflects the theme of kindness and the rewards of compassion. Even the huntsman spares Snow White out of pity.

Resilience and Survival – Despite the queen's repeated attempts on her life, Snow White survives each time, showing resilience and the capacity to endure hardships.

Justice and Retribution – In the end, the queen's envy leads to her downfall, suggesting that malicious actions eventually bring about their own punishment.

Love and Redemption – The prince's love for Snow White breaks the spell of death, reinforcing the idea that love has the power to redeem and revive.

These themes reflect the timeless moral lessons embedded in the tale, emphasizing virtues like kindness, humility, and the eventual victory of good over evil.

SNOW WHITE'S CHARACTER

Snow White's character in "Little Snow White" by the Brothers Grimm is defined by several key traits:

Innocent and Pure – Snow White embodies innocence, which is evident in her trusting nature. She accepts gifts from the disguised queen despite the dwarfs' warnings, reflecting her naivety and lack of suspicion.

Kind and Gentle – Snow White's kindness shines through her interactions with the dwarfs. She gratefully accepts their hospitality and offers to cook, clean, and care for them in return.

Beautiful – Her physical beauty is central to the story, described as having skin "as white as snow, lips as red as blood, and hair as black as ebony." This beauty incites the queen's jealousy and drives the plot.

Trusting to a Fault – Snow White's trusting nature makes her vulnerable. Despite being warned, she repeatedly falls for the queen's tricks, such as the poisoned apple and comb. This highlights her innocence but also suggests a lack of worldly experience.

Resilient and Strong – Though she faces several assassination attempts and even falls into a death-like sleep, Snow White ultimately survives and thrives. Her endurance and ability to overcome adversity demonstrate quiet strength.

Forgiving and Compassionate – Snow White shows no bitterness or desire for revenge against the queen, reflecting a forgiving heart. This underscores her moral purity and capacity for compassion.

Symbol of Goodness – Snow White's character serves as a contrast to the queen's vanity and malice, embodying the triumph of goodness and virtue over evil.

Overall, Snow White is a classic representation of virtue and innocence, whose story serves as a moral lesson about the dangers of envy and the rewards of kindness and love.

THE QUEEN'S CHARACTER

The queen in "Little Snow White" by the Brothers Grimm is a complex character driven by negative traits that propel the story forward. Her personality can be summarized by the following characteristics:

Jealous and Envious – The queen's defining trait is her overwhelming jealousy of Snow White's beauty. Her envy intensifies as Snow White grows more beautiful, leading her to attempt murder multiple times.

Vain – The queen's obsession with her appearance is reflected in her constant need for validation from the magic mirror. Her desire to be the "fairest of them all" shows her superficial and self-absorbed nature.

Deceptive and Manipulative – The queen repeatedly disguises herself (as a pedlar, an old woman, and a peasant) to deceive Snow White. Her cunning and ability to deceive others highlight her manipulative tendencies.

Ruthless and Cruel – The queen's willingness to kill a child to secure her status demonstrates her cruelty. She resorts to extreme measures, such as poisoning Snow White with a comb and an apple, without hesitation.

Determined and Relentless – The queen does not give up easily. Even after her initial attempts fail, she continues plotting to eliminate Snow White. This persistence underscores her deep obsession and single-minded pursuit of her goal.

Prideful and Arrogant – The queen's pride prevents her from accepting that anyone could surpass her. This arrogance blinds her to the possibility of failure, ultimately leading to her downfall.

Tragic and Self-Destructive – In the end, the queen's jealousy consumes her. When she discovers that Snow White is alive and now a queen, her rage and envy overwhelm her, resulting in her collapse and death. This reflects the destructive nature of envy and hatred.

The queen serves as a cautionary figure, illustrating the dangers of vanity, jealousy, and unchecked ambition. Her character is a stark contrast to Snow White's innocence and virtue, reinforcing the story's moral lessons about the consequences of envy and the eventual triumph of goodness.

THE SEVEN DWARF'S CHARACTERS

The seven dwarfs in "Little Snow White" by the Brothers Grimm are not individually distinguished by unique personalities in the original tale. Instead, they collectively represent certain shared characteristics:

Kind and Hospitable – The dwarfs take Snow White into their home without hesitation. They offer her shelter and protection in exchange for her help with household chores.

Protective and Caring – They care deeply for Snow White's well-being, warning her repeatedly not to let anyone in while they are away. Their protective nature reflects their loyalty and affection for her.

Hardworking – The dwarfs are miners, spending their days digging for gold and silver in the mountains. Their dedication to their work symbolizes industriousness and perseverance.

Perceptive and Wise – The dwarfs are quick to recognize danger. After the queen's attempts on Snow White's life, they are suspicious and cautious, immediately identifying the cause of Snow White's collapses (the lace, the comb, and the poisoned apple).

Compassionate and Gentle – When they believe Snow White is dead, the dwarfs mourn her deeply, watching over her for days and refusing to bury her because of her preserved beauty. Their compassion highlights their emotional depth.

Honest and Fair – The dwarfs are straightforward in their dealings with Snow White and the prince. They refuse to sell Snow White's glass coffin for gold but eventually relent out of pity for the prince's love.

While the dwarfs are not as individualized as in later adaptations, their collective character plays a crucial role in protecting and caring for Snow White, embodying virtues of kindness, diligence, and loyalty.

SUMMARY OF THE STORY

In the middle of winter, a queen pricks her finger while sewing and wishes for a daughter with skin as white as snow, lips as red as blood, and hair as black as ebony. Her wish is granted, and she names the child Snow White. Tragically, the queen dies, and the king remarries a vain and jealous woman who owns a magic mirror.

The new queen constantly asks the mirror, *"Who is the fairest of them all?"* and is pleased when it tells her she is. However, as Snow White grows, the mirror proclaims her beauty surpasses that of the queen. Enraged, the queen orders a huntsman to kill Snow White. The huntsman, unable to harm the innocent girl, spares her life, and Snow White flees into the forest.

She finds refuge in the home of seven dwarfs who take her in. They warn her not to let anyone in while they are away. However, the queen, discovering through the mirror that Snow White still lives, disguises herself and attempts to kill her three times—first with a tight lace, then a poisoned comb, and finally with a poisoned apple. The apple causes Snow White to fall into a death-like sleep.

Believing her dead, the dwarfs place Snow White in a glass coffin. One day, a prince sees her and falls in love. As the prince's servants carry the coffin, they stumble, dislodging the piece of apple from her throat, reviving her.

The prince and Snow White marry. The wicked queen, upon learning Snow White is alive and now a queen, collapses from rage and envy, leading to her downfall. Snow White and the prince live happily ever after.

Moral: The story highlights the dangers of vanity, jealousy, and the inevitable triumph of innocence and goodness over evil.

THE BROTHERS GRIMM'S TECHNIQUES – FORM AND STRUCTURE

The Brothers Grimm employed several distinctive techniques, forms, and structural elements in *Little Snow White* that contribute to the tale's lasting appeal and effectiveness as a fairy tale. Here are the key aspects of their storytelling approach:

Form and Structure:

Simple, Linear Narrative
The story follows a straightforward, chronological structure. Events unfold in a clear sequence:

- Snow White's birth and her mother's wish.
- The queen's envy and the huntsman's mercy.
- Snow White's refuge with the dwarfs.
- The queen's three attempts to kill her.
- Snow White's revival and marriage to the prince.

   This simplicity makes the tale easy to follow for both children and adults.

Repetition and Rule of Three
The queen attempts to kill Snow White three times — with the lace, the comb, and the poisoned apple. This repetition builds tension, reinforces key messages, and mirrors common oral storytelling traditions.

Symbolism and Motifs
Key objects and descriptions (e.g., the magic mirror, poisoned apple, glass coffin) carry symbolic weight, enriching the narrative with deeper meanings related to vanity, innocence, and mortality.

The colours white (innocence), red (life and danger), and black (mystery and death) reappear throughout the tale, reinforcing themes of duality and transformation.

Contrast of Good and Evil
The stark contrast between Snow White and the queen highlights the battle between innocence and malice, a hallmark of Grimm's fairy tales. Snow White's purity and kindness consistently oppose the queen's vanity and cruelty.

Character Archetypes
The tale features classic archetypes:
- The Innocent (Snow White) – Represents purity and virtue.
- The Villain (The Queen) – Embodies envy and malice.
- The Helpers (The Dwarfs, Huntsman, Prince) – Protect and guide the heroine. These archetypes create a moral framework that is easily recognizable across cultures.

Moral and Didactic Elements
The story conveys moral lessons about the destructive nature of envy and vanity. The queen's downfall serves as a cautionary tale, reinforcing the idea that evil is ultimately self-destructive.

Magical Realism and Transformation
Magic is seamlessly woven into the fabric of the tale (e.g., the talking mirror, the queen's disguises, Snow White's revival), reflecting the Brothers Grimm's tradition of blending reality with fantastical elements to convey moral truths.

Minimal Characterization
The Brothers Grimm use minimal description and dialogue, relying on archetypal roles rather than deep psychological exploration. This brevity allows the audience to project their interpretations onto the characters.

Happy (or Poetic) Justice Ending
Like many fairy tales, "*Little Snow White*" concludes with justice and resolution. Snow White is rewarded for her goodness, while the queen's envy leads to her downfall, reinforcing the theme that good ultimately triumphs over evil.

Oral Tradition Influence
The story's repetitive structure, simple language, and moral focus reflect its roots in oral storytelling. The Brothers Grimm preserved the essence of folk tales, making them accessible and engaging for readers of all ages.

In summary, the Brothers Grimm crafted "*Little Snow White*" with a blend of symbolism, repetition, archetypal characters, and moral clarity, creating a timeless and universally resonant story.

GLOSSARY OF LITERARY TERMS

Snow White (Character) – The protagonist, a young princess with skin as white as snow, lips as red as blood, and hair as black as ebony. Her beauty makes her the target of the queen's envy.

Queen (Stepmother) – The antagonist, Snow White's vain and jealous stepmother. Obsessed with being the fairest in the land, she attempts to kill Snow White multiple times.

Magic Mirror – A mystical object the queen consults to determine who is the fairest. It speaks the truth, driving the plot forward by informing the queen that Snow White surpasses her in beauty.

The Seven Dwarfs – Small, hardworking miners who take Snow White into their home and protect her from the queen. They represent kindness, loyalty, and diligence.

Poisoned Apple – A deadly fruit the queen uses in her final attempt to kill Snow White. One side is harmless, while the other is poisoned, leading Snow White to fall into a deep, death-like sleep.

Disguise – A recurring motif where the queen disguises herself (as a pedlar, old woman, and peasant) to deceive Snow White.

Cottage – The home of the seven dwarfs where Snow White finds refuge after fleeing from the queen.

Glass Coffin – A transparent coffin crafted by the dwarfs to preserve Snow White's body after they believe she is dead. The coffin symbolizes Snow White's purity and unchanging beauty.

Prince – A noble figure who discovers Snow White in the glass coffin. His love and intervention (moving the coffin, causing the apple to dislodge) lead to Snow White's revival and their eventual marriage.

Envy – A central theme representing the queen's driving force. Her jealousy over Snow White's beauty leads to the story's major conflicts.

Betrayal of Innocence – Snow White's trusting nature allows the queen to harm her multiple times. This theme highlights the vulnerability of innocence in the face of deception.

Resurrection – Snow White's revival after the poisoned apple dislodges from her throat. This symbolizes rebirth, hope, and the triumph of good over evil.

Symbolism of Colors –

- White (Snow White's skin) – Purity and innocence.
- Red (Blood) – Life, love, and danger.
- Black (Ebony hair) – Mystery and strength.

Moral of the Story – A lesson that highlights the destructive nature of envy and the eventual victory of innocence, love, and kindness over malice and vanity.

ABOUT THE AUTHORS – 'THE BROTHERS GRIMM'

The Brothers Grimm, Jacob Grimm (1785–1863) and Wilhelm Grimm (1786–1859), were German scholars, linguists, and folklorists best known for their collection of fairy tales. Their work has had a profound impact on Western literature and culture.

Background and Early Life:
Born in Hanau, Germany, Jacob and Wilhelm were the eldest of six siblings.
After the death of their father, the brothers pursued higher education at the University of Marburg, where they studied law but developed a passion for linguistics, literature, and folklore.

Contributions and Achievements:
Fairy Tale Collections:
Their most famous work, "Children's and Household Tales" (1812), commonly known as *Grimm's Fairy Tales*, compiled traditional German and European folk stories.

The collection included famous tales such as:
Snow White
Hansel and Gretel
Cinderella
Little Red Riding Hood
Rapunzel

The tales were originally intended for academic preservation but gained popularity as children's stories. Over time, they softened some tales' darker themes to appeal to younger audiences.

Linguistic and Academic Contributions:
The Grimms were pioneers in German philology and contributed significantly to the study of the German language.

Jacob Grimm formulated Grimm's Law, a foundational theory in the development of Indo-European languages, describing sound shifts in early Germanic languages.

They worked on the German Dictionary (Deutsches Wörterbuch), an ambitious project documenting the German language, though it was incomplete at the time of their deaths.

Cultural Preservation:
The Grimms believed that folk tales and language were vital to preserving national identity and culture. Their work helped foster a sense of German unity and pride during a time when Germany was fragmented.

Legacy:
The Brothers Grimm are celebrated worldwide, with their stories forming the basis for numerous adaptations in literature, film, and theatre.

Their fairy tales continue to inspire modern storytelling, influencing modern authors today.

In 2005, UNESCO recognized their original manuscripts as part of the Memory of the World Register.

The Brothers Grimm are remembered not only as storytellers but also as key figures in the preservation of folklore, shaping the way we understand the cultural heritage of Europe.

Printed in Great Britain
by Amazon